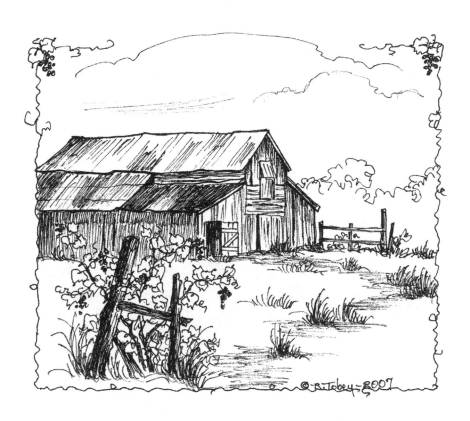

From the Scribbles and Sketches Collection

Written and Illustrated by

RUBY TOBEY

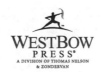

WESTBOW
PRESS®
A DIVISION OF THOMAS NELSON
& ZONDERVAN

Scripture quotations taken from the New American Standard Bible® (NASB), Copyright © 1960, 1962, 1963, 1968, 1971, 1972, 1973, 1975, 1977, 1995 by The Lockman Foundation Used by permission. www.Lockman.org

Scripture quotations marked (NIV) are taken from the Holy Bible, New International Version®, NIV®. Copyright © 1973, 1978, 1984, 2011 by Biblica, Inc.™ Used by permission of Zondervan. All rights reserved worldwide. www.zondervan.com The "NIV" and "New International Version" are trademarks registered in the United States Patent and Trademark Office by Biblica, Inc.™

WestBow Press books may be ordered through booksellers or by contacting:

WestBow Press
A Division of Thomas Nelson & Zondervan
1663 Liberty Drive
Bloomington, IN 47403
www.westbowpress.com
1 (866) 928-1240

Because of the dynamic nature of the Internet, any web addresses or links contained in this book may have changed since publication and may no longer be valid. The views expressed in this work are solely those of the author and do not necessarily reflect the views of the publisher, and the publisher hereby disclaims any responsibility for them.

Any people depicted in stock imagery provided by Thinkstock are models, and such images are being used for illustrative purposes only. Certain stock imagery © Thinkstock.

ISBN: 978-1-9736-1710-5 (sc)
ISBN: 978-1-9736-1711-2 (e)

Library of Congress Control Number: 2018901067

Print information available on the last page.

WestBow Press rev. date: 02/09/2018

Dedicated to all the Tobey Tribe
(my husband, children, and grandchildren).
You helped make me what I am, and you are
a precious part of all my life.
Even though we don't get to be together
Often, we are united in love.

Preface

Ruby Tobey records life in a sketchbook. When she was raising three children, there wasn't always time to paint, but sometimes she would make a quick sketch. She filled many sketchbooks with drawings of homey farms, country scenes, mountains, wild flowers, and roadsides wherever the family traveled. She still makes those sketches whenever she can, in her own backyard or on travels with children and grandchildren. Ruby feels that sketching and painting in nature makes one even more aware that God is there and he is the master creator.

The material in this book was taken from a devotional newsletter Ruby does in connection with her work as an artist.

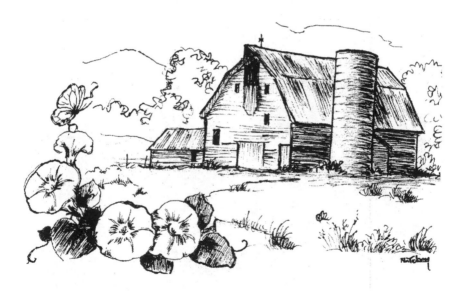

Artist's Despair

I see tall trees on a mountainside,
Feel the stirring pulse of the ocean's tide.
I see green fingers of a flower's leaf,
Wheat-covered land in a golden sheaf.
I see shadows in the willow's lace;
See subtle colors on a canyon's face,
I see wind patterns on a grassy plain,
Then my hopes dissolve in frustration and pain.
Neither brush, nor pencil, nor ink and pen
Can capture this beauty, so once again,
I'm disheartened with hopes I'll never fulfill
And awed by my God's creative skill.

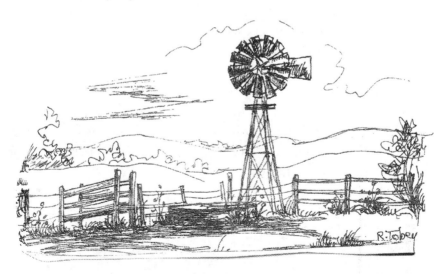

Get It Over With

I like the warm days we often have to break up our winter here in the plains area. After a couple of weeks of cold, dreary days, it's nice when the temperature warms up for a few days. But I never want the warmth to last long. I have the theory that we have to have a number of cold, wintry days, so let's just get them over with. My husband, Joe, has another philosophy. He says each warm day is just one less cold day.

I realized I had this "get it over with" thinking about a lot of things. If I had to learn some hard thing, if I had a hard situation dealing with people, or even a hard project with my art, I just wanted to get it over with and enjoy life again.

I'd really like it to be that way, have all the hard things, grit my teeth, face it, get it over, and not have to think about the hard part ever again.

But life doesn't come like that. When you've gotten over a hard patch and rested, another problem comes along. When you think you've learned all there is about dealing with people, another situation arises. When you've learned to do your job well, something changes, and you have to start over.

I'm making progress in learning to live with the ups and downs of life, to enjoy the sunny days without worrying about what may come later. I'm not in control, but I can let God have control. I can trust him to help me when the cold, dreary days come again.

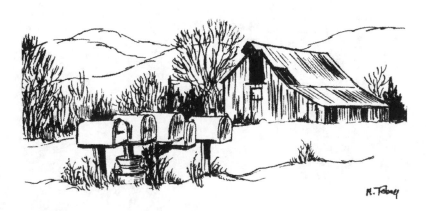

R. Tobey

This is the Day That the Lord Has Made

The sunrise is so beautiful
As it touches each thing in gold,
Awakening a sense of wonder,
Almost more than my heart can hold.
And I am glad and unafraid,
For this is the day the Lord has made.

Now problems begin to worry me
And storms start to gather about,
Ending the day in confusion
As my mind is tortured with doubt.
But I will be glad and unafraid
For this is the day the Lord has made.

I am learning to walk each day,
To accept any kind of weather:
The pattern of life is woven
From the good and the bad together.
So I am glad and unafraid
For this is the day the Lord has made.

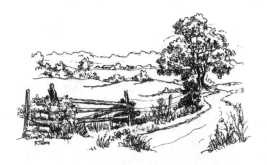

Along a country road in Virginia

This is the day the Lord has made; we will rejoice and be glad in it.
(Psalm 118–24, NIV)

Help Someone

We know as we give we shall receive
but it's not so easy to achieve.
Forget yourself and really believe
you can help someone.

Others do good we neglect to mention,
If we can give them our love and attention,
our own lives will take on new dimension
as we help someone.

There are those who need help everywhere,
spend time thinking of them in prayer.
Just reach out and show them you care;
Help someone.

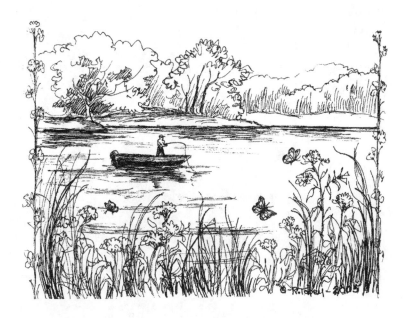

Butterflies were enjoying the wild flowers along
the shore of a lake near Wichita, Kansas

Let no unwholesome word come out of your mouth, but only what is helpful for building others up according to their needs that it may benefit those who listen. (Ephesians 4:29, NIV)

This is one of those verses that jumped out and hit me in the heart. I've had to work hard to practice it. It's so easy to forget and think about what I'm feeling and what I need.

We hear a lot about problems of low self-esteem. I heard one speaker say that we could not have good self-esteem unless we were doing something to build it instead of dwelling on our own feelings and failures.

Applying the above verse of scripture is the best way of doing something for others. Encourage people. Everyone is so busy and hurried and involved. Everyone of us has our share of struggles and problems and heartaches. No one is immune from them. So smile and encourage people, and above all, pray for others.

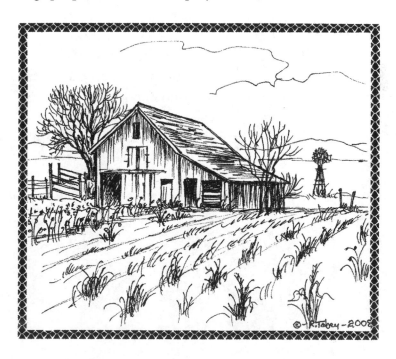

Old barn near Lindsborg, Kansas.]

Problems and Suffering

We all have problems and suffering. What we do with what happens is the important thing. Ask, "What can I let God do with this?"

In spite of how terrible or how hopeless it seems at the time there are some good things that come from these problems. For one thing, it helps us find our priorities. We realize most of the things we get upset about don't really matter. Being close to God matters, other people matter. It's easy to get involved in too many things. When these changes happen, we are able to drop what doesn't count and realize what things we really need and value.

Remember gold is refined by heating, which melts out the impurities. Problems in life work on us the same way. So even the hard, difficult things we go through make us grow stronger.

Make the best of where you are. When I was a teenager, I was working away from home for the summer. I didn't always get to go home on the weekends, and I would get so homesick I could hardly make it through the week. One night I opened my Bible and discovered Philippians 4:11. I like the entire fourth chapter, but that verse has been a favorite since that night. It reads "Not that I speak from want, for I have learned to be content in whatever circumstances I am" (NAS)

Sometimes all we can do is be content until our circumstances change.

God is our refuge and strength, a very present help in trouble. (Psalm 46:1 NAS)

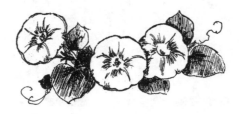

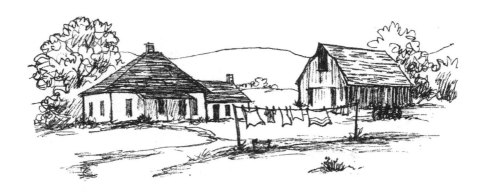

A farm south of St. Francis, Kansas]

It's takes both rain and sunshine to make a rainbow.

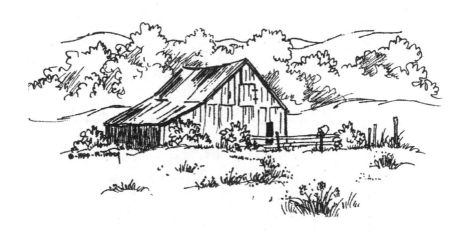

My Lord Is Taking Care

The Lord is taking care of me I know,
although it doesn't really always show.
I wonder often when problems are there,
when my heart is burdened and heavy with care,
when my friends face trials that I can't understand
and sorrow forms a veil that hides His hand.
Though my thoughts tempt me to give up and leave,
my faith hangs on and tries to believe.
Then I'm awed at the way He uses things for good,
and it works out in ways I never thought it could.

"We know that in all things God works for the good of those who love him, who have been called according to his purpose" (Romans 8:28, NIV).

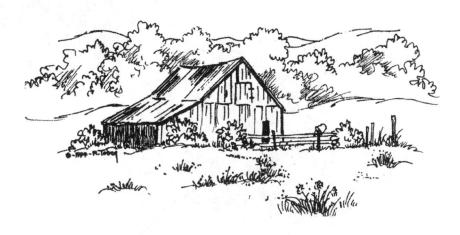

Barn near Crane, Missouri

Life's Changes

As I was planning this fall newsletter I re-read the devotional page I had sent out last spring. I found several statements in my article that now apply to me.

One statement was "when our lives change suddenly..." and another, "when these changes happen we are able to drop what doesn't count and realize what things in our life we really need and value." Then there was, "we realize most of the things we get upset about don't matter."

When I wrote those thoughts I didn't realize how much of it would apply to me in a few months. I'd had a few of those experiences; now I've added a few more.

I had never had nor expected to have any major surgery. When it was my turn, I was reminded again that our lives can change in ways we don't expect.

We hear about problems and tell people we will pray for them, and we do for a while. Sometimes it gets to feeling like just a saying until it's our own turn to need those prayers.

How good it is to know then there are others thinking about us and praying for us!

Life is so busy and it's easy to get rushed and forget about others. Remember to take time to *pray* for those you know who need it; then let them know of your concern with a card. (Remember, someone who is ill may not feel like talking on the phone but can read a card any time and more than once.)

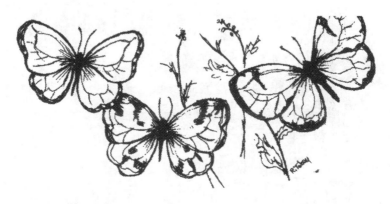

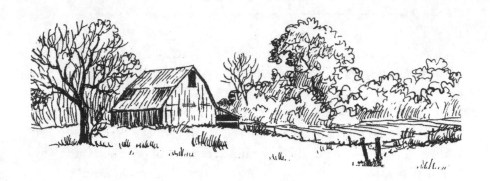

near Springdale, Arkansas

Be anxious for nothing, but in everything, by prayer and supplication,
With Thanksgiving, let your requests be made known to God.
(Philippians 4:6, NAS)

The prayer of a righteous man is powerful and effective. (James
5:16, NIV)

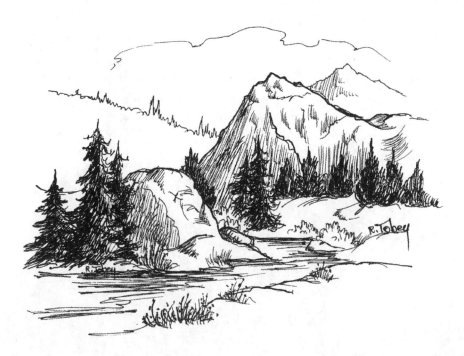

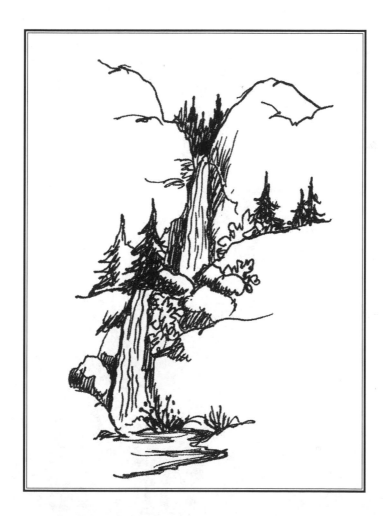

Eleven Mile Canyon near St. George, Colorado

Thank You for Prayer

Father, I thank you
For the comfort of prayer,
For healing my heart,
For just being there.
I was wrapped up in cares,
Both imagined and real,
And life's daily challenge
Had lost it's appeal.
Then I remembered to stop
And restart my day,
Take my mind from myself,
And kneel down to pray.
Now, Father I thank you
For the comfort of prayer.

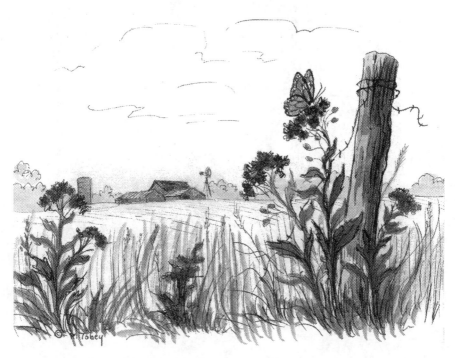

Cleaning and Sorting

After Christmas, I spent some time going through shelves in the basement. It's where I store some of my supplies. There was white china waiting to be painted. There were craft supplies from past projects and books and sewing odds and ends.

I tried to be ruthless and eliminate the things I don't use, can't use, or have no more interest in using. Some was donated to charity collections, and some went to the trash. And I discovered some treasures I'd forgotten that I can now take out and use.

Life is like my experience with cleaning. Every so often, we need to clean and sort what is going on in our lives. There are probably some bad habits we need to recognize and eliminate. There might be some laziness creeping in that could be changed. Possibly there are things we might discover that we could put to better use. Maybe there is a talent we haven't been using to help other people. We might find some time we could use to visit someone who needs it. Often we have been selfish and kept things we could share such as our time and our money.

Then too we might find a real treasure that has been covered over with the clutter that accumulates when we are so busy and on the go.

The beginning of a new year is the traditional time to take stock and reorganize our lives. But any time is a great time to stop and see where you've come from and where you are going.

And He said to them "beware, and be on your guard against every form of greed; for not even when one has an abundance does his life consist of his possessions."
(Luke 12:15, NAS)

Love Seeds

I have many plans for what I'll do
in giving care and helping too.

I think of friends I love so much
and lonely people I need to touch.

But time goes by and needs aren't met,
I get so busy I just forget.

My thoughts of kindness are the seeds,
but love only grows with words and deeds.

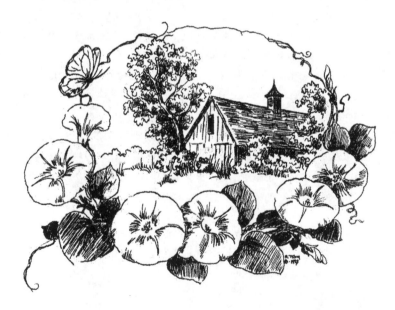

Morning glories frame a sketch of a barn near Halstead, Kansas

I pray that you may enjoy good health
and that all may go well with you,
even as your soul is getting along well
(3 John 1:2, NIV)

Work the Plan

Discipline yourself for the purpose of godliness.

—1 Timothy 4:7 NAS

A year ago, I had serious health problems and wasn't sure for a while what the future would be. After surgery took care of my low blood sugar problems, and things returned to normal; I thought I would do more worthwhile things with my life. I have been grateful for the return of my health, but I'm still working on doing better things with my life.

It's easy to think about things I'll do, but not easy to make plans and really do them. Have you ever thought about having someone over, but you didn't make the phone call, so it never happened? Have you ever thought about something you could do for someone, but you decided to wait awhile, then got busy and forgot? Have you ever felt swamped with other things and put off making a phone call to cheer up someone? Or how about starting to improve your Bible study, then never getting back to it? I've been guilty of doing all those things.

As the above scripture says, "discipline yourself." That is the key—discipline. It doesn't happen with good thoughts, as I wish it would. There has to be a plan. There has to be work.

I hope you are making progress with discipline. Change comes slowly, a little at a time.

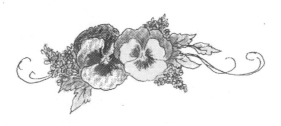

You will seek me and find me, when you search for me with all your heart. (Jeremiah 29:13) NAS

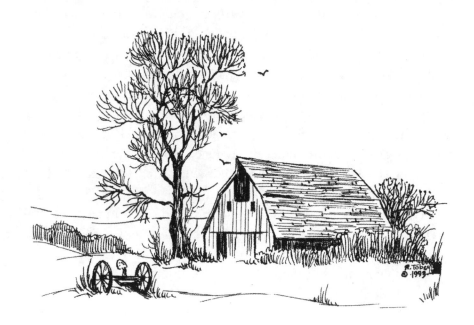

Life Under Construction

From the beginning of life to the end,
there's a process we all go through
as we are under construction.
We're building with all that we do.
The days pass by so quickly.
But they will determine whether
our habits are concrete to strengthen
and hold all our plans together.
If you are discouraged with routine
or because you feel unskilled,
then turn your life to the master,
and follow his lead as you build.

Trust in the Lord with all your heart and do not lean on your own understanding. (Proverbs 3:5, NAS)

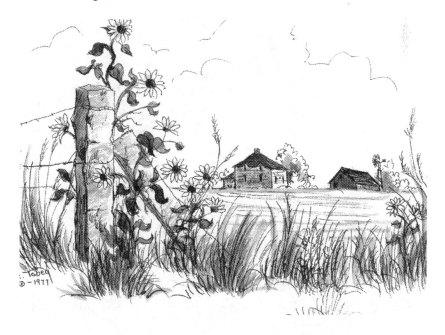

A stone fence post near Wilson, Kansas

Attitude of Gratitude

Rejoice always, pray without ceasing, in everything give thanks, for this is God's will for you in Christ Jesus.

—1 Thessalonians 5:16–18, NAS

In my newsletter, I mentioned making a trip to Texas. After the rains stopped and we drove to Northeastern Texas, we saw so many pretty flowering trees. The roadsides were green, and there were lots of daffodils blooming. Our spring here in Kansas comes a few weeks later, so I was grateful for the taste of early spring.

I may have written about being grateful before, but it is so important that I need to be reminded often. Gratitude includes the word "attitude," and that's what it is: *a grateful attitude.*

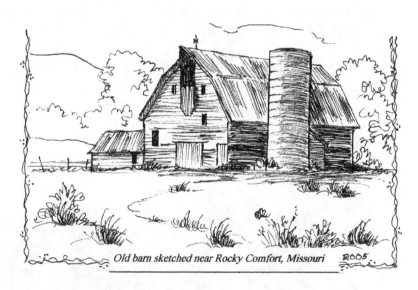

Old barn sketched near Rocky Comfort, Missouri 2005

Old barn sketched near Rocky Comfort, Missouri.]

I will give thanks to the Lord with all my heart. (Psalm 9:1, NAS)

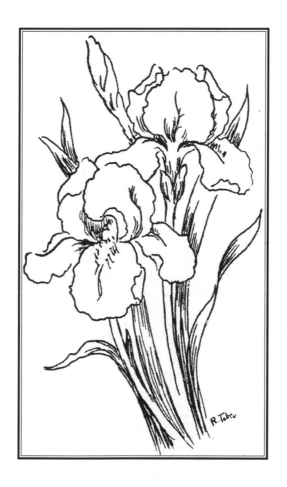

Your Gifts

Forgive me for taking for granted
your very gracious gifts to me.
So many precious things there are,
like friends and home and family.
Each day I am flooded anew
with another bountiful supply,
and I often forget to thank you
as the time goes fleeting by.
Would you keep your patience with me?
For I've been ungrateful I confess.
Lord, I do know you're the giver
of all that I have to possess.

One writer suggested that we take time at the end of each day to list five things for which we are grateful. This takes a little discipline to actually make yourself sit down and write, not just think about it. Usually, if you do start to list things for which you are grateful, the list grows. As you do this often, you begin to concentrate on the good that happens. It's especially encouraging if you are living with problems right now or if you have illness. It may be a challenge, but you will find there are still some good things in each day.

Don't just feel grateful; take time to give thanks for those good things. Even better, if there are people who have contributed to these good things in your life, take time to tell them how grateful you are for them and for what they have done for you. Then, they as well as you, will have more good things in life, and the *attitude of gratitude grows and grows.*

Trusting God

How often do we try to solve our own problems instead of waiting for God's help? When we were in California a few years ago our van overheated. We were driving toward Yosemite National Park and anxious to get there. First, we put all the water we had with us in the radiator. After driving a short distance, it boiled out. Next, we got out our little camp stove and melted all the ice in our ice chest to get more water. After we put that in the radiator, we only made it a short distance before the van overheated again.

I had prayed for God's help, of course, but we were busy working it out ourselves. The third time, we found some water in a ditch at the bottom of the hill. We climbed down the hill and filled all the cooking pots we had with us. Then we had to strain the dirty water through paper towels into the radiator. It took two trips to get enough water, and we made it less than a mile before we were stranded again.

By that time, we were stuck and out of new ideas. Then a tow truck passed us on its way back from another call. The driver stopped to help, and we were soon towed back to town. It wasn't the direction we had planned to go. But the faulty thermostat was soon replaced, and we were on our way again. It was a day and a half later when we made it to Yosemite. But our van was running well, and we had new friends and new memories.

Isn't that how life works sometimes? We try everything we can think of to make things turn out our way and on our schedule. When things look hopeless and we've exhausted our own resources, the Lord lets things work out for us. Maybe they work out with a delay, maybe not in the direction we wanted to go, but in ways we never thought possible.

Trust in the Lord with all your heart, and do not lean on your own understanding. (Proverbs 3:5) NAS

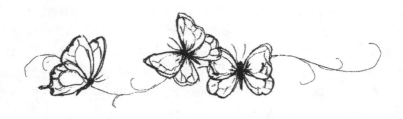

Oh give thanks to the Lord, for He is good; for His loving kindness is everlasting. (Psalm 107:1, NAS)

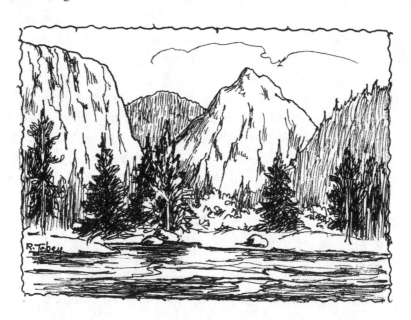

Along the Merced River in Yosemite National Park

Majesty

How noble and how grand,
how great is your power, Lord,
creator of the universe,
who is loved and adored.

Your majesty is seen
displayed up in the sky
whenever summer rains bring out
the rainbow up on high.

Awesome beauty seen on
the mountain and the plain,
and your power is expressed in
the storm clouds and the rain.

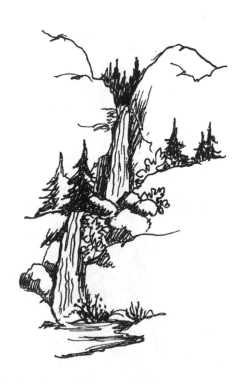

Count Your Blessings

I woke up late on a dark, dreary morning. It looked like it could be a cloudy, depressing kind of day. But when I opened the curtains, things looked brighter. It wasn't as dark as I'd thought, and soon the sun came out and brightened the whole world.

Isn't that the way our days go sometimes? Our thoughts are dreary and depressing. Maybe we're thinking of the hard things we have to do that day or sad things that happen in this world.

Sometimes we're even reluctant to change our thoughts and let the light in. But something happens to focus the sunshine: a friend calls, a special letter arrives, and things start to look better.

When my husband's sister, Eileen Grey, became paralyzed on one side as a result of a brain tumor, we were amazed that she kept going so well. Even though she could not even get herself in and out of her wheelchair, she kept busy sending cards to other people, typing letters with her one good hand, and reading. When we asked how she stayed so cheerful, she said, "This is not the way we had our life planned. We have pity parties, but we give ourselves fifteen minutes to feel sorry. Then we get back to life."

And so it is, we can think of the hard job we have to do that day or we can be glad we are able to do it. We can moan about the cold and windy weather or we can be glad we have a warm place inside. We can be unhappy and lonely because we think our friends don't care or we can take time to reach out to them.

It's like that cloud parting and the ray of sunshine coming through. Our thoughts can be full of hope and sunshine. But sometimes it takes a lot of effort on our part. And it's much easier for me to write about it than to do it.

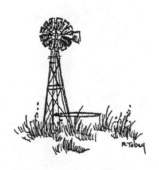

Help me know contentment,
To be at peace,
That my endless worries
May find release.
Help me see the good I have
Here all around.
Let me forget problems
As blessings are found.
Just for today I ask,
Hear me I pray,
Keep me under your care,
Don't let my thoughts stray.

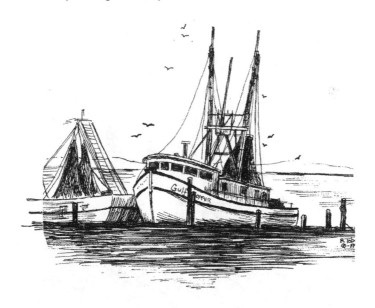

Shrimp boats along the Gulf Coast of East Texas

And my God will supply all your needs, according to His riches in Christ Jesus. (Philippians 4:19, NAS)

Time

How often we panic
and try to compare
plans we weave
with what we achieve,
It only adds to our care.

It passes so quietly,
And then time moves on:
Laughter, tears,
Days into years.
Turn around, and it's gone.

Time moves by so quickly.
It's gone in a wink.
What we do,
Showing love too,
Means much more than we think.

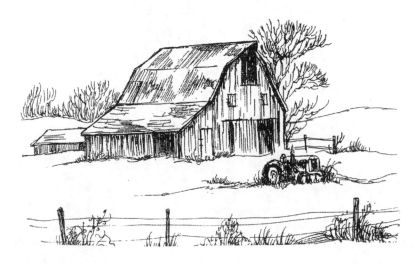

A Missouri barn in Winter

Just Thinking about Time

Most of us think about time every day: how fast it goes, how much we have, how little we get done. Ecclesiastes 3 talks about a time for every purpose under heaven. But some days it feels like there isn't time for anything or any purpose.

I have mentioned our trips to the War Eagle craft fair in Arkansas. One of our sons and his family come over every year to spend time with us at the fair. The first trip our granddaughter Kara made to the fair was when she was five months old. Time passed and soon she was old enough to help wrap items as I sold them. Now, she is taller than I am and likes to do some shopping as well as help me in my booth. We have good memories of those times, but it's still amazing that time has passed so rapidly.

I'm sure you can think of similar things in your life and find it hard to believe time has passed so quickly. The recent death of two long-time friends reminded us again of time and memories.

Time will speed by no matter how you use it. But memories are precious, so enjoy your life and your friends. Make as many good memories as you can.

But as for me, I trust in You, Oh Lord. I say," you are my God. My times are in your hand." (Psalm 31:14–15, NAS)

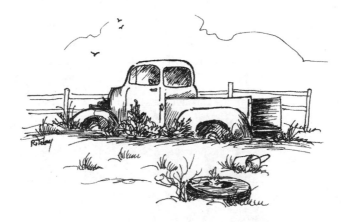

Sketched on a cousin's farm in Washington state

You Can't Direct the Wind, but You Can Adjust Your Sails

One February day, we drove out to the lake to do some walking. We noticed a man in a kayak paddling down the lake. Soon he was headed back to the other end of the lake. This time we really took notice because it was a very windy day, and the waves he was facing looked dangerous.

We watched for a while. At times the kayak seemed to disappear between the big waves, but it always appeared again and seemed to be making slow progress against the rough water and wind.

We finished our walk, and I settled down to make a sketch of some trees. In a few minutes, my husband said, "The boat has capsized!" The man was hanging onto the kayak, and the rough waves were washing over him. We raced our car around the lake and found someone who was calling the rescue services.

He did gradually drift to shore and into shallow water. He was too exhausted to climb out, and the rescue workers had to help. He was soon being warmed up in the rescue vehicle.

We kept asking, "What was he thinking of? Why was he taking such a chance on a cold, windy day?"

But we often do the same. We think we can get close to danger, and it won't affect us. We might listen to gossip, thinking we can refrain from taking part, but it's easy to slip into that habit ourselves. We might neglect our body thinking it won't matter, but problems can show up later. We even go places we know we shouldn't be, always sure it won't be a problem.

We always think we can handle what comes and that nothing bad will happen to us. Sometimes it's good to look at the mistakes of others and learn from them.

A wise man is cautious and turns away from evil; but a fool is arrogant and careless. (Proverbs 14:16, NAS)

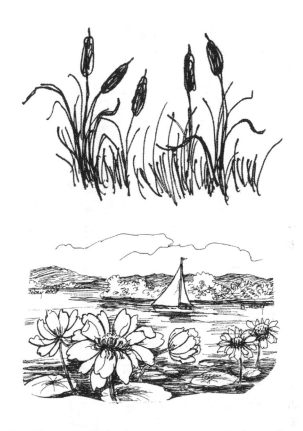

Let the Lord be mindful of me; you are my help and my Deliverer.
(Psalm 40:17, NAS)

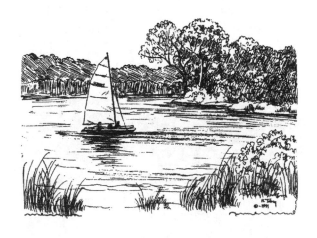

Sailing on Arcadia Lake near Edmond, Oklahoma

A Helping Hand

Encourage the fainthearted, help the weak, be patient with everyone.

—1 Thessalonians 5:14, NAS

Last spring, I wrote about watching a man in a kayak at the lake. He was paddling against the waves on a day when the wind was strong and the waves high. Eventually he capsized. Even though he was able to hang onto his boat and fight the waves, he eventually needed help to get out of the lake.

I likened this to the way we are sometimes when we think we can go against common sense or do risky things and not get in trouble.

But there is another lesson here.

We need to notice when others have problems and might need a helping hand. We need to be willing to help and not judge whether they got themselves into the difficulty. We're usually so busy with the things we need to do that it is easy to overlook the needs of others. Sometimes they just need you to be there for them. Sometimes you may need to listen to their problems. You could be the only person who can help.

Also, we are often the one in trouble, either by our own making or just the way life goes. When that happens, we need to admit we need help. If we need a friend, if we need help or need a favor, we must ask for it. Forget pride or embarrassment, and let someone else lend us their strength. If the man in the kayak had done that, he could have saved himself much struggling in the cold water and the risk of losing his life.

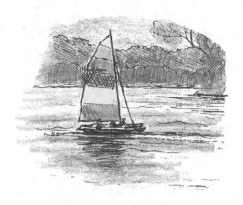

Give a Smile

Give a smile to someone,
and be sure they know you care.
Give your time to someone.
When they need you, just be there.
Share your joy with someone
if you find there is a need.
This life was made for laughter;
only you can plant the seed.
Share your wealth with someone,
whether yours is great or small.
It was meant for sharing,
for you cannot keep it all.

And do not judge and you will not be judged; and do not condemn and you will not be condemned; pardon and you will be pardoned. Give, and it shall be given to you; good measure, pressed down, shaken together, running over, they will pour into your lap. For by your standard of measure it will be measured to you in return.
(Luke 6:37–38, NIV)

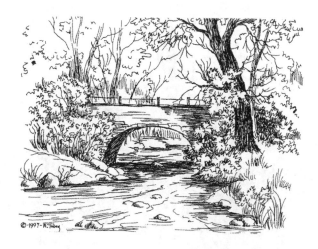

Bridge in Cimarron Canyon, New Mexico

31

The First Day of Spring

It was the first day of spring with snow on the ground.
Its chilly white softness lay spread all around.
There should have been sunshine instead of the gloom,
There should have been green grass and fruit trees in bloom.

But there was a lesson, for I looked in my heart
And found discord and coldness and love kept apart.
There should have been happiness waiting to show,
There should have been caring and love all aglow.

So I checked on my habits, on my thoughts put a guard,
And I worked every day, and I tried very hard.
The seed kept growing from one little start.
And now it's the first day of spring in my heart.

Finally brethren, whatever is true, whatever is honorable, whatever is right, whatever is pure, whatever is lovely, whatever is of good repute, if there is any excellence and if anything worthy of praise, dwell on these things. Philippians 4:8 NAS

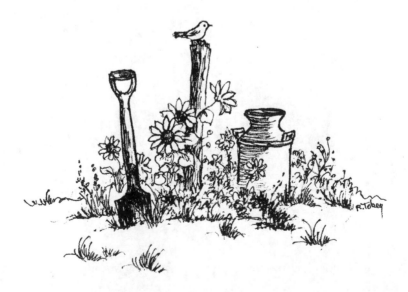

Our Values

One of the most important principles of art is to learn to get the values right. We mean the lightness or darkness of the colors or shading when artists talk about values. I have a book titled, "Tonal Values, How to see them - How to paint them." If you have a good arrangement of light and dark values you can tell what a picture is even in a dim light or from a distance.

"Get your values right" can apply to life also. If you're sure of your values, life works well. In this sense values means -- right and wrong, good and bad, what is worthwhile versus what is worthless.

Then when the way seems dim, when you aren't sure what to do or which way to go, you can remember the values in your life. If you already have them in place, it's easier to do the right thing.

In art, teachers say to get the values of your colors right, and the picture will have shape. Then you can put in all the details later. In life, put your good values in order and apply them; then you can take care of the details involved. We could write a book titled *Life Values—How to See Them, How to Live Them.*

If you have always tried to do what is right, you don't have to decide between right and wrong in a situation. You won't be easily confused when a choice presents itself. You can decide on the right decision and then take care of the details. When we have our values right and the picture is clear, living life day to day is easier.

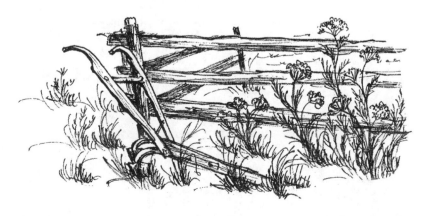

The Nature of Talent

*And to one He gave five talents, to another ten, and to
another one; to each according to his ability.*

—Matthew 25: 15, NIV

Of course, I love it when people say I'm talented. But I've always
believed the saying that talent is 10 percent inspiration and 90 percent
perspiration. Being interested enough to do lots of practice and lots of
work makes a big difference.

Aside from art, we all have things we can do well. My friend Evelyn
bakes wonderful pies—something I've never done well. And my niece,
Sandy, sews beautifully. Corrine and Carol are two of my friends who
have the ability to make people feel special, and I know they encourage
lots of people. And Elaine, who does the typesetting for this newsletter,
has computer skills I'll never learn. I can think of many more, and each
one is special and different.

I could probably be better at any of those things with more practice.
I still couldn't do as well as these friends do because they have that extra
touch, which we like to call talent.

Don't ever think you can't do anything or have no talent. What you
can do is useful and important and can mean a lot to other people.

I'll finish up by using a portion of two different Bible verses:

So then, while we have opportunity let us do good to all people.
(Galatians 6:10, NAS)

Whatever your hand finds to do, do it with all your might."
(Ecclesiastes 9: 10, NAS)

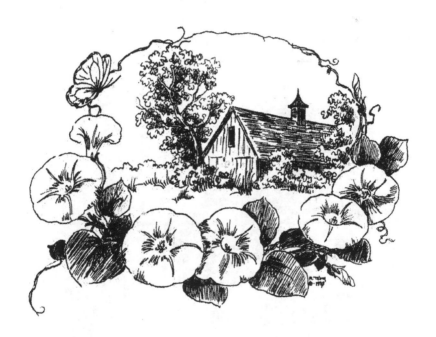

Talent

You think you've no talent, nothing you can do,
But I know you better. I know it's not true.
Your talent may be simple like cleaning or sewing.
Not painting or writing but maybe just knowing
How to be friendly—just what to do,
To put someone at ease, or encourage them too.
Your talent's valued by God. It's needed here now.
He'll help you use it. He'll show you how.
You may never win praise in the eyes of man,
But you have a place in the Master's plan.

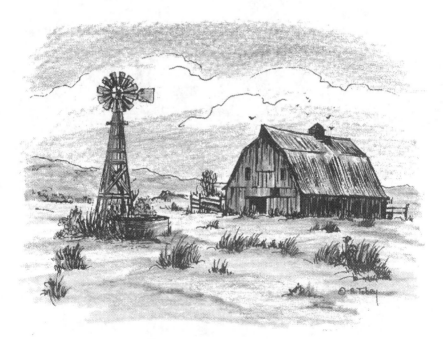

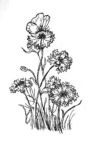

Prayer is like a butterfly,
a softly moving thing,
lifting words to heaven,
up by a fragile wing.
A quiet talk with God,
setting the thoughts free,
fluttering from the heart,
the soul's unspoken plea.
A cocoon for the mind
to reshape and renew.
Time spent in silent prayer
changes our earth-born view.

And do not be conformed to this world, but be transformed by the renewing of your mind. (Romans 12:2, NAS)

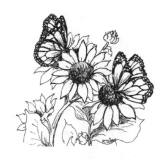

Transformation

Butterflies have always been a favorite of mine. It's always amazing to watch them on the flowers I grow.

How can such fragile wings carry them? How can Monarchs migrate so many miles? How could God design so many intricate wing patterns? How can something as ugly as a caterpillar transform into a beautiful butterfly?

They have been described as "jewels of the garden," and they really are!

Thinking of the transformation of the caterpillar always gives me hope. It is compared to the transformation we go through after death, and it fits that picture.

But I also think it fits life now. It gives me hope that I can change and grow into a more tranquil person. Maybe if I spend more time, as they do, among the beauty that surrounds me, the change would be easier.

We are bombarded with bad news, bad talk, and all the sordid things we can be exposed to day in and day out. We have to work hard to spend time feeding on the good.

One of my favorite Bible passages is below:

Whatever is true, whatever is honorable, whatever is right, whatever is pure, whatever is lovely, whatever is of good repute, if there is any excellence and if anything worthy of praise, let your mind dwell on these things. (Philippians 4:8, NASV)

This verse gives me hope that the work I do with painting is worthwhile, and it also keeps me striving to transform my thoughts, deeds, and ideals into someone who glorifies God.

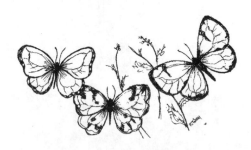

Changes

Life is full of changes. There is an old saying that the only thing you can count on is change.

I prefer to write checks, to remind me that I'm spending money, but stores now would rather use your bank card.

I finally learned not to pound the keys so hard and was getting along with an electric typewriter when along came computers on the scene; one barely has to touch those keys. Now they take over many of the typing and printing jobs we used to do.

I spent years learning china painting. Painting on china with specially formulated paints, then firing the piece in a kiln. Then painting and firing again to get deeper colors. Now there is a paint for china and glass that just needs to be heated in your kitchen oven. Although I don't think the effects you get with these paints are as pretty, it's another change.

For years, you could only paint watercolors on paper; now there is a canvas for watercolors. As well as the art field, there are changes in all areas. As soon as you get used to one thing, technology gives us another. Our cars are different, our music is different, appliances are different, jobs are phased out, and things are replaced and changed every day.

We want to get to the place where things are comfortable, and we can depend on things being the same. But life is always changing. Maybe that is good, because then we cannot rely so much on what we have and what we can buy. All the fast changes can remind us to focus on the things that last: our families, our friends, our relationship with God.

A couple of lines from a poem I wrote in the past express it,
"Change to change time passes,
and things get out of style,
we need to do the things
that really are worthwhile."

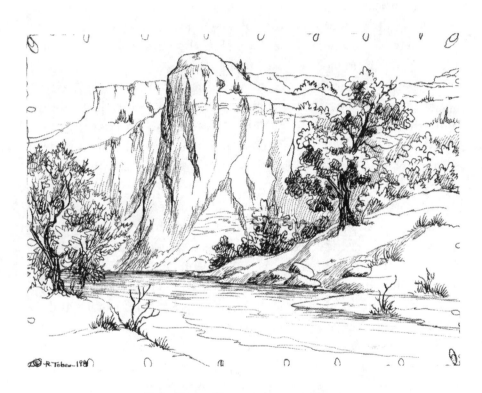

Palo Duro Canyon in west Texas

Time Marches On

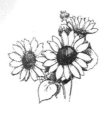

I see the change of seasons;
Time quickly marches on.
Today I plan for things I'll do,
But tomorrow time is gone.
So many pleasures beckon,
Things I want to see and know,
If only time would wait for me
Instead of rushing so.
But in my rush and hurry,
With a schedule to get through,
I must find time to stop, dear Lord,
And spend some time with you.

But seek first His kingdom and His righteousness and all these things will be added to you. Matthew 6:33 NAS

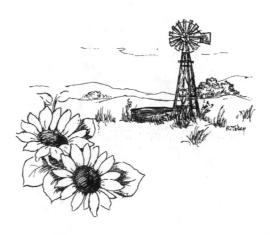

Teach Me

Every day you show me,
now I'm beginning to see
how my thoughts are often
thinking only of me.

I know I want to change,
to think of other's needs,
but everything in this world
just nurtures selfish seeds.

I'm going to need your help, Lord,
it'll take some pain and strife
to turn my thoughts to caring
and learn a new way of life.

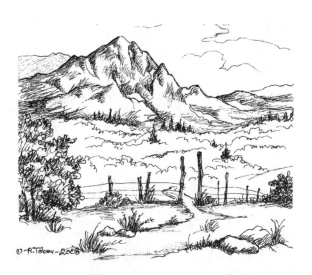

Along the Dallas Divide west of Ridgeway, Colorado

It was such exciting chaos to have all our children and grandchildren together in our small house for the weekend. And there were many kind things done for us and so many fun experiences all at once. It would have been great to stretch it out and have more time to enjoy each thing. But life doesn't work that way. It is often so busy with so many things to enjoy and to take care of all at once. When that happens, it leaves us little time to think of others.

Now that things have slowed down, I've had time to remember each good thing. And I am reminded that little things we do for other people do make a difference. Those acts remind us that we do matter to other people. In the average daily routine, everyone has times when they feel alone and forgotten. I've been guilty of thinking it didn't matter because what I could do was so small. Stopping to send a card or make a call doesn't seem like much, but it means a lot to the person on the receiving end.

Thinking on these things reminds me to take time from myself and do more for others. And I need to do it sometimes just because I care and not because of a special occasion. Sometimes I have to have the experience before I realize the difference it makes.

Maybe I've learned a little from this, but like the old saying goes, "We are too soon old, and too late smart."

Always seek after that which is good for one another and for all people. (1 Thessalonians 5:15, NAS)

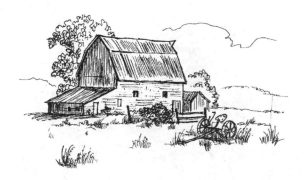

Barn on a farm near Aurora, Missouri

Keeping Life in Balance

I have probably written on this before—it seems to be one of the struggles in my life. Keeping life in balance. There are so many options, so many things going on.

If I work more, can I keep up at home? When I spend time painting, do I neglect doing what I need to do for others? If I don't spend time painting, will I be frustrated? Do I need to drop out and find time for the important things? Should I spend more time with friends? Do I take time getting to know my grandchildren better or talk more with my children and spouse? And how do I find time for all the things I need to do or want to do? We could spend hours trying to find answers to these and other important questions and thoughts.

Life passes by so quickly, and I constantly get bogged down with all the things I want to do, versus all the things I need to do, versus all the things I think I need to do. Then I realize I've neglected to do things for others because I was so busy planning how to do it all.

With one of our family members gravely ill and the long illness of a sister-in-law, my thoughts turn again to the really important things. I wake up and resolve to do better with the time I have in my life.

I just read this statement, "Will the things I plan even matter a year from now?" Ouch! I am reminded to give love and encouragement and help to others whenever I can. I need to be reminded again and again that things aren't always the best use of time.

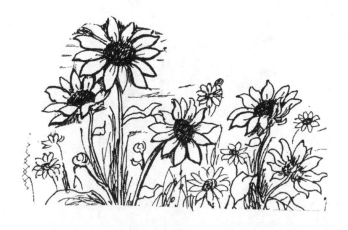

Sharing

What is life not lived for others?
What does it count when all is done?
What joy do you gain from your days
If you save them up one by one?
When you take them out of your memory,
To view when time has passed by,
What moments will shine with brightness?
Will those deeds make you smile or cry?
For you reap whatever you sow,
What you give will come back to you.
Don't wait and find your life empty
When your time of sharing is through.

He who sows sparingly will also reap sparingly and he who sows bountifully will also reap bountifully. (2 Corinthians 9:6, NAS)

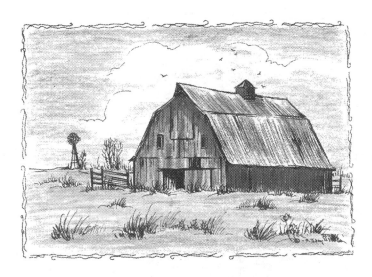

We Hope Winter Is Past

I've always liked the verse in Song of Solomon 2: "The Winter is past, the rain is over and gone, the flowers appear on the earth, the time of singing of birds is come."

Spring always makes us feel better, the warmth after the cold, more light after the short days, and the green of new life showing in plants. We are not quite at that point of spring as I write this. Our up and down weather makes me think it will be awhile before we can say, "The winter is past." Just recently, we had lots of seventy-degree days in February. Then the first of March, it was freezing again, then back to warm weather again in the same week.

Some of my daffodils were blooming almost four weeks early. Things looked very spring-like. Then the temperature dropped back into the teens. When I looked at those flowers, they were lying over on the ground. But even though they didn't look good, I know they will bounce back in time.

All this makes me think how life is. Things are going great, life is easy and smooth, then the freeze comes in the form of sorrows, pain, and other trouble. We get knocked down, and for a while, things don't look so good. Sometimes it takes a lot of time and tears and effort to bounce back. It can seem endless when we are going through it, but the time of the singing of birds will come again. With time and faith and maybe a long wait, flowers will bloom again in our lives.

This is written with the hope that your winter is over and gone. If it isn't, have faith that the happy times and the blooming of your life will come again.

Cast your burden upon the Lord, and He will sustain you. (Psalm 55:22, NAS)

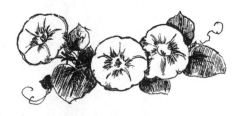

Pain

Now it's my time to be sad and blue
For pain comes to everyone, it's true.
Though I don't want to face it, I must;
It's hard to hold on to hope and trust.
Time drags by when I want it to hurry
And bring an end to this ache and worry.
Others help, but I'm still alone.
Just being lost and on my own.
But even when these things hurt so much,
I still can feel God's loving touch.

See! The Winter is past; the rains are over and gone, flowers appear
on the earth; the season of singing has come,......Song of Songs 2: 12 NIV

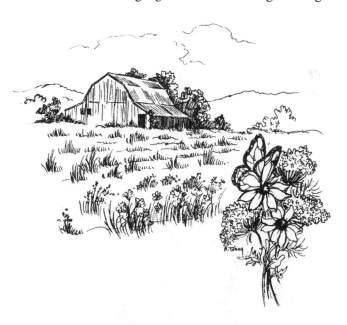

Country roads were lined with wild flowers when
I sketched this barn in northern Kentucky

Elderly

And even when I am old and gray, O God, do not forsake me.

—Psalm 71:18, NAS

I've never liked the term "elderly." I've seen it used in the newspaper to describe people I think are still young.

Several years ago, I wrote a poem titled "Elderly Ladies." It was the result of people seeing my artwork and thinking I must be elderly because I often painted old barns, windmills, etcetera. And the term "elderly" was not always used in a flattering way.

Now that I am an "elderly lady," I've reviewed my reasons for writing that poem.

The people, not just ladies, who have reached that age group have a lot of strength. They have faced heartaches and problems in the past. They have survived and grown stronger because of that. Many have lost mates and loved ones. They've had problems with children or helped care for grand children. Some have had their hearts broken by tragedies and still come back to face life. In spite of aches and pains, they are still doing and loving and sharing with others.

I've had to deal with some of those things but have not attained those virtues yet, but their example gives me hope that I can keep on growing.

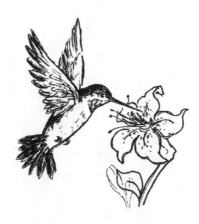

Grow Old with Beauty

Grow old with beauty.
Seek it everywhere.
In a wonderful play.
In a soft-spoken prayer.
In all of nature,
The rivers and mountains.
In city places
Like flowers and fountains.
Look for it in others
And find out their best.
Then you'll always have beauty
And be richly blest.

Light is shed upon the righteous and joy on the upright in heart.
(Psalms 97:11, NIV)

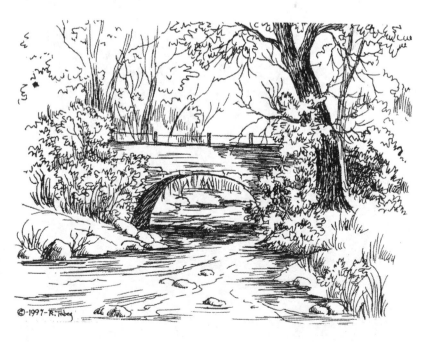

Elderly Ladies

Sometimes when I meet someone who knows my name but not my face
They expect an elderly lady and exclaim as if it's a disgrace.
Then we both smile and forget it, but later, I stop and find
There must be something about me, a more sober frame of mind.
But is it bad to be a lady with an old-fashioned point of view?
And how about these other things, I know the world could use them too:
Patience, kindness, faith, and endurance when life's drear
So a cheer for elderly ladies! They're beautiful and dear.

But as for me, I trust in you, O Lord.
(Psalm 31:14)NAS

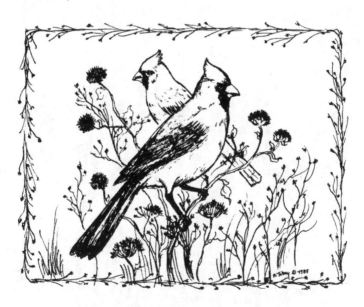

Slow Me Down

Slow me down I cannot do
All the things that I want to.
Slow me down so I will see
When others have a need for me.
Show me who needs loving kindness;
Take away my selfish blindness.
Slow me down when I rush so,
Help me take the time to grow,
In life's busy, restless maze.
From my swift and careless ways.

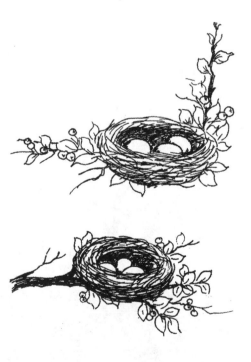

For the Lord is good; His loving kindness is everlasting.
(Psalm 100:5, NAS)

Take Time

I've always wanted to do more things than I have time for, so I keep moving. And when I was raising three children, I needed to. I wanted to find time for painting as well as mothering.

But I do have a tendency to plan one thing after another and get so busy I forget to look around. I forget to see who else might need my time. I forget that I don't have to do it all because there is "a very present help in trouble."

Time has taken care of slowing me down so I can't rush as much as I used to. Although my husband still complains that I walk through a room fast enough to create a cold wind, I don't seem to get as much done. When I ran across this poem I'd written some time ago, it meant something to me again.

I still need to be reminded to take time for people. Painting is important to me but is not always the best use of my time.

God is our refuge and strength, a very present help in trouble. (Psalm 46:1) NAS

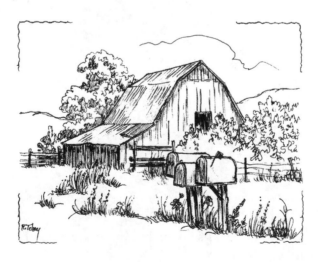

Barn along a country road west of Guion, Arkansas

Take My Advice

If any of you lacks wisdom, let him ask of God, who gives to all men generously, without finding fault, and it will be given to him.

—James 1:5, NIV

I don't get to see all of my six brothers and sisters as often as I'd like. But about once a year, we all get together for a reunion at our hometown. We always try to spend as much time as we can together. And of course, the conversation always turns to our children and grandchildren.

One of them was talking about a situation in a child's life and a suggestion they'd made about how to solve it. Then they added, "They don't really want our advice. They want to do it their way." And we'd all had that experience with raising children.

The next day, one of my sisters said she'd been thinking that's how God sees us. We have his word to show us how to live. He knows what's ahead and what's best for us. He knows the dangers of our own way. He wants to help us, and yet we don't ask. And that's because we want to do it our own way. We're like those children who get into trouble and cause themselves problems by doing it their own way. When will we learn to trust Him?

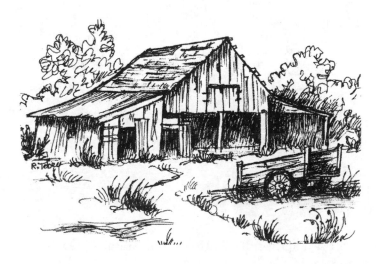

The old barn on the place where we all grew up at Milton, Kansas

Words

Wrong words, careless words,
bring hurt and dismay.
When busy, not thinking,
they're easy to say.

Speak well, speak kindly.
How do you know
who needs you, who's hurting,
struggling as they go?

Your kindness, your love,
might be all they need
and encouragement; uplifting,
can grow from a tiny seed.

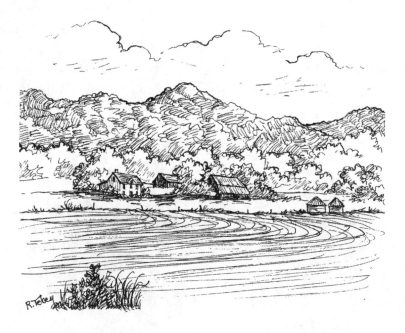

Along the hills South of Council Bluffs, Iowa

Murphy's Law/Tobey's Law

You've heard of Murphy's law (if anything can go wrong, it will go wrong). Well, I have two laws of my own.

Tobey's law number 1 is, "No one ever comes by when the house is clean." Have you noticed? You keep the house picked up and fairly clean all the time. Then one day, you're extra busy, things go wrong, and you don't stop to pick up the clutter. That's the day someone drops by. It's usually someone you don't know well, so it's not as easy to relax and forget it. But you might as well for that's life.

And Tobey's law number 2 is, "Your possessions expand to fit your storage space." Have you noticed? When you buy more shelves, another shed, more things to organize, it seems like you are all set. The next thing you know, all that storage is full, and you're looking for another place to put things.

Having an interest in how our homes look and having the desire for things is normal. But they can get out of control and take too much of our time and money. That is when we've gone too far.

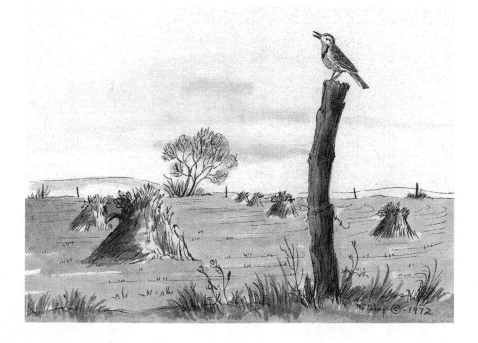

Distractions

What a constant barrage of sights and sounds and scenes,
All working to get my attention by almost any means.
So many sweet surprises to see and feel and touch,
So many charming temptations to try and do too much.
But there are quiet moments within the constant call,
Sometimes I hear a small voice rising above it all.
So then I am reminded of what is all worthwhile,
And I find the strength to resist the over-full life style.

Then He said to them "Watch out! Be on your guard against all kinds of greed; a man's life does not consist in the abundance of his possessions." (Luke 12:15, NIV)

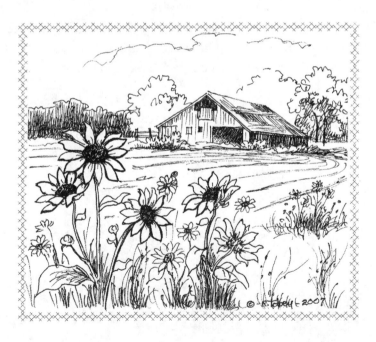

A barn near Harper, Kansas

Friends

There are different kinds of friends, but they all add to your life and leave their mark. There are casual friends who are always fun to be with. There are friends who are around awhile, and life changes, and they move on. But they leave a memory to enjoy. There are a few close friends that you can really share your heart with. They're always there to rejoice and enjoy when times are good. They are there to support you when times aren't so good. You can help them when their bad times come, and you have to learn to let them help you when you need it. That's all part of friendship.

There are lifelong friends. You've both supported each other through problems. Maybe your lives are so busy that you don't see them often. Just knowing they've always been there and you've shared so much means more and more as time goes by.

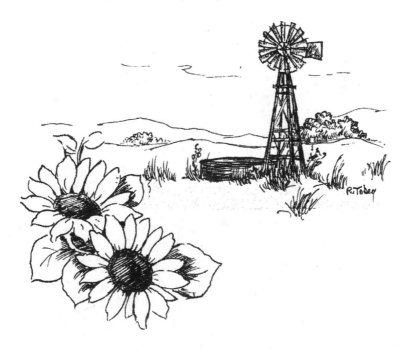

Friendship

Friendship is a special trust:
A tie between two friends,
A cord between kindred hearts,
A chain that never ends.

It can help each person grow:
To weather any storm,
To know there's always someone close
Whose heart is strong and warm.

So treat each friend like a gift,
A precious jewel you've found.
Express your care in loving ways
That keep you closely bound.

A friend loves at all times. (Proverbs 17:17, NAS)

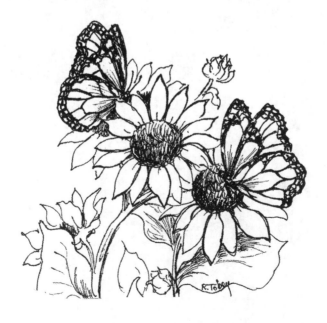

And More Friends

When we got together with school friends recently, I thought of how the years have changed us. When we were young and in school, and even when we were young adults, it was different. Most of us thought about our own interests. We had hang-ups and fears. We worried more about how we looked and how we fit in.

But the years have passed, and we have lived life. We have raised families and struggled with jobs. The years have brought losses, disappointments, and even health problems.

Now, when we get together, we are more supportive and caring of one another. It means a lot to share memories, and we miss those who are gone. We are so happy to see each other and we laugh and hug and realize what friendship means.

What a blessing it is to have friends. Give thanks for all of them, and don't forget to show them you care.

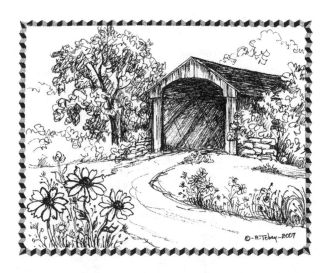

Wildflowers bloom around a covered bridge Near Versaille, Indiana

In everything give thanks. (1 Thessalonians 5:18) NAS

The Year of the Bunnies

This was the year for bunnies—painting them, talking about them, and seeing them around. It started last spring when we noticed a rabbit sitting in my flower bed. It was there several days, and we realized it had a nest there. I was able to take a photograph of that bunny sitting in the purple and blue flowers. And one Summer evening, we watched four young rabbits running and playing in the grass across the street from our house. They were so cute.

A couple of times neighborhood cats sat watching our yard. I scared them away to protect the rabbits.

Even this winter, there was often a rabbit sitting near the bushes when I went to the front yard. It seemed to like being near people as long as we didn't make any sudden moves.

And then we had a big snowstorm. There was a rabbit around. We assumed it was the same one we'd been seeing. It sat near Joe and kept him company while he shoveled. Everything was covered in snow, so I put out some vegetable scraps for the rabbits, but none of it was eaten.

Then the bunnies reminded me of how we often are. God is near but we don't trust him enough. We are afraid to let him help us. We don't want to sit still long enough to get close to him. We don't want to feed on what he has for us. He protects us, and we don't realize how much is done for us. Like the bunnies, we ignore what is there.

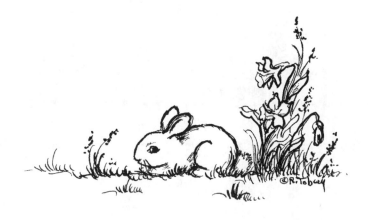

Comfort

There's a great sense of peace
That means so much,
As I kneel in prayer
And feel His touch.

The safety in knowing
I can come here,
That the care of the Lord
Is always so near.

And the feeling of home:
Comfort and rest,
The strength in knowing
I am so blest.

He has made everything beautiful in it's time. He has also set eternity in the hearts of men: yet they cannot fathom what God has done from beginning to end.
(Ecclesiastes 3:11, NIV)

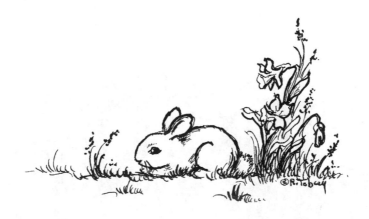

Season Of Life

Is not wisdom found among, the aged? Does not long life bring understanding? (Job 12:12, NIV)

I was talking with one of my sisters about the fall colors coming in the trees. Many of the maples were turning red, and other trees were starting to show yellows and oranges. Fall can be a great time with its brisk temperatures, colorful trees, and warm campfires. But it is always a little sad and melancholy to see summer end, and winter getting closer.

Sometimes life is compared to the seasons of the year. We are young in spring; the summer comes with middle age, and life is good and our bodies are healthy and strong. Then fall comes, and we start to see the changes.

Like the rich harvest and the warm colors of fall, the autumn of life can be a lovely time. I have many friends who are also at that time of life, and I can see that they have grown warm and loving and beautiful in spirit.

The poem I am using on this page is one I wrote when I was still in the summer of my life. I had been talking with an older friend who made the statement that nobody wanted to get older, but we all want to live a long life.

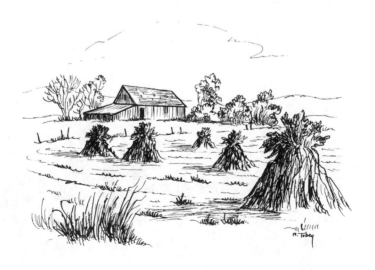

Fall sketch made near Marquette, Kansas

Everyone Wants to Live Longer; No One Wants to Get Older

We all want to be happy,
long life is our ambition,
but growing older is
such a strange position.

This world of ours has become
very conscious of age.
It is a false measure
that we use as a gauge.

For just think of what it means
when birthdays come and go;
growing older is a gift,
it really is, you know.

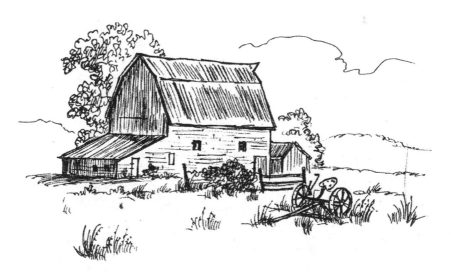

To God Our Daily Thanks

My friend, Corrine, calls now and then just to see how I'm doing. I like her attitude because she almost always talks about how blessed she is and how thankful she is for her family and all she has. And even though she's getting older she can still do many things.

When we talked this summer, she mentioned something her preacher said in one of his sermons. It went something like this: if you want to have a good day, give thanks when you get out of bed and can still move. Then count your blessings and go out and do something for someone else.

It's a simple thought, but one I need to be reminded of often. It's so easy for me to get too busy. Suddenly I realize how much time has gone by without me doing anything for anybody else.

It may have lost something in the process of converting it to my thoughts. And working to make the rhymes and rhythms forced more changes. But I thank a minister in Ada, Oklahoma, for the reminder. I'll try a little harder to apply it.

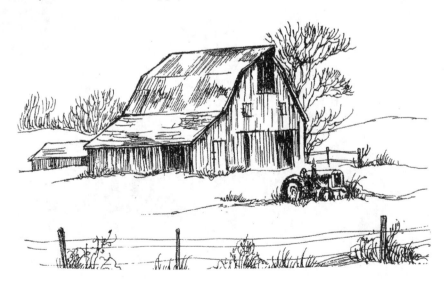

Recipe for Good Days

To start each day give thanks,
For health, for all life sends.
Be grateful for each gift,
Family and special friends.
Just look around and see
The birds and butterfly wings.
And don't forget to count
All nature's little things.
Then when you list it all
And turn to start your day,
There's one more thing to think of
Before you go your way.
Let God show you where to go
And who might need your care,
Share some time with someone.
You'll find great happiness there.

Let us not love with words or tongue but with actions and in truth.
(1 John 3:18, NIV)

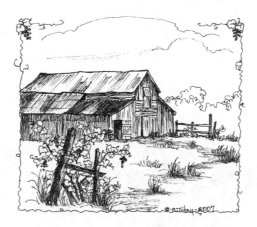

Even the wild grapes were through for the
season near this old barn in Arkansas

The Technology Age

I am from the wrong generation to really embrace technology. To me it is a necessary frustration. I'm not only being forced to use it but just when I learn how to use programs, they upgrade or change them and I have to start again. And I have noticed... the times we live in make it hard to be still. It's even harder when we have so many technologies and gadgets that keep us in touch with everything.

One day I saw a mother and her daughter at the park. The mother was pushing her girl on the merry-go-round. But she was facing away from her and lazily pushing as she talked on the phone. She was paying very little attention to her child.

You've seen the people walking on the street and not looking where they were going because they are checking the screen on their phone. Or the people in the restaurants who don't relax and pay attention to their companions. They're busy talking on their phone or checking for messages.

We are so used to almost constant noise and entertainment that it is hard to slow down and sit quietly. We are even that way with our families who should get our best attention. It is hard to be quiet and focus on the important.

So it is even harder to stop and concentrate on what our spirit needs. It takes work to sit quietly long enough to pray, to study God's word, or to meditate on the lasting things in this life.

In quietness and trust is your strength, but you were not willing. (Isaiah 30:15) NAS

In Quietness

Jesus often went apart to meditate and pray;
Alone in the garden He found strength to obey.
Could this be the reason for much inner strife,
The unrest and problems, no joy in this life?
Do possessions and pleasures soon start to pall?
Do you sometimes grow weary of facing it all?
Come apart for a moment, away from the throng.
Let the peace of His presence make your heart strong.

Be still and know that I am God. (Psalm 46:10) NIV

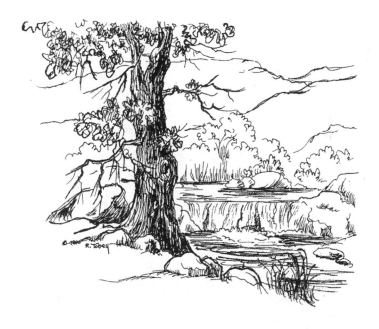

This tree sketch was made while we were on a
hike in the Grand Canyon in Arizona

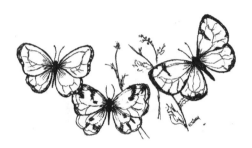

A portion of proceeds from this book will go to charity:

To Christian Relief Fund of Amarillo, Texas -- to help with poverty and disaster relief around the world.

To American Farmland Trust – which works to preserve our farmland and help farmers remain on the land. I chose them because I grew up in farm country and have used many sketches of farms in the book.

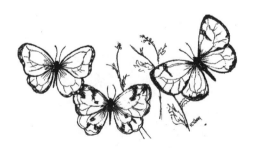

Printed in the United States
By Bookmasters